Spirit
in the
City

Spirit in the City

The Angels and Elementals of Wicca

Tudorbeth

Tudorbeth © 2013

All rights reserved.
No parts of this publication may be reproduced, stored in a retrieval system, or transmitted in any form or by any means whatsoever without the prior permission of the publisher.

A record of this publication is available from the British Library.

ISBN 978-1-907203-87-9

Typesetting by Wordzworth Ltd
www.wordzworth.com

Cover design by Titanium Design Ltd
www.titaniumdesign.co.uk

Printed by Lightning Source UK
www.lightningsource.com

Cover images by Nigel Peace

Published by Local Legend
www.local-legend.co.uk

*Dedicated to my father, whose love of legends
and our history brought him home and sent
me on a life-long journey of discovery
of our ancient knowledge.
Blessed Be, Dad, may you be at peace
forever in the Summerlands.
Love, light and peace to all in spirit.
Thank you for your grace.*

Blessed Be to all.

The Author

Tudorbeth is a hereditary practitioner of the Craft. The rules and gifts of herb lore, scrying, healing, tasseomancy, numerology and candle magic have been passed down to her through several Celtic and English generations. Born in Wiltshire, she has an Honours degree in Religious Studies and has lived and worked in California and Italy, before returning to live in north London.

Previous Publications

The Craft in the City (ISBN 978-1-907203-43-5)

The Witch in the City (ISBN 978-1-907203-63-3)

Spells in the City (ISBN 978-1-907203-70-1)

Magic in the City (ISBN 978-1-907203-81-7)

Published in paperback and eBook by Local Legend

www.local-legend.co.uk

Contents

Introduction	1
Angels	3
A Glossary of Angels	9
Axis Mundi	13
Doppelganger	19
Dragons	23
Elves	27
Fairies	31
The Lady of the Lake	37
Leprechauns	41
Merfolk	45
Mothman	49
Nymphs	53
Pegasus	57
Phoenix	59
Pixies	65
Salamanders	69
Serpents	73
Sphinx	77
Unicorns	81

Vampires	85
Werewolves	91
Conclusion	97
The Festivals and their Elementals	101
Other Magical Beings of Spirit	103

Introduction

Dear Reader,

Witches work with the spirit and the elementals of nature all the time in our different festivals and rituals, to show our gratitude and to seek help with healing and with spells. The elementals referred to here are ones that we most often work with and ones that our family members may know of or have seen. So there is a personal connection with them in one form or another.

These elementals of spirit would have been accepted without question many years ago. The last century saw huge belief in fairies and angels, for example, and the atrocities of World War I especially brought many belief systems to the fore. There were many cases around those times, such as the Cottingley fairy photographs of 1917[1], which had the support and backing of Sir Arthur Conan Doyle who was a firm believer in the existence of fairies.

But the early twenty-first century is very different and the way of life is vastly changed from a hundred years ago. Rapid urbanisation and the almost total destruction of the old ways of life has brought change to such an extent that the past and its belief systems seem completely alien to us now. In those days people had no television, no computers or Internet, even little electricity

---

[1] Cottingley is near Bradford in England. Cousins Elsie Wright, aged 16, and Frances Griffiths, aged 9, published five photographs apparently showing fairies. In the 1980s they finally admitted that four of them were faked, but still claimed that the fifth was genuine.

to speak of. The cinematic age was just in its infancy, as was the idea of flight let alone space travel and landing on the moon. People still travelled by horse and cart as the motor car was a luxury only the elite could afford. Many people grew their own food in their gardens and women still fought for the vote. People simply could not imagine how different the world would become.

Look how far we have travelled in a hundred years. Many of the common superstitions and beliefs of those times would be scoffed at now as science has dismissed many of them.

Yet the existence of the elementals, beings of energy, prevails in our technologically pioneering world. Those of us who work in the realm of spirit are aware of these elementals. Further, we welcome them into our lives and work with them wherever we can for the benefit of all. To work with spirit and to be a part of the world of magic, you need to let the elementals in and allow yourself to believe…

In many of the forthcoming letters, a number of semi-precious stones and crystals will be mentioned. However, please do not go to great expense to practise magic or to connect with spirit. The only important resource that is ever really needed is YOU. The stones and crystals can help us manifest spirit within the physical world; the two that are all-rounders and perfect for anything in this work are clear quartz and amethyst.

One of my favourite sayings regarding gem stones is from the Lakota Sioux: "The outside of the stone is round; the power of the stone is endless."

And so are you. The power, the magic and the spirit that resides in you is endless. Through this series of letters we shall look at other aspects of spirit. We shall learn to acknowledge, harness and respect their energies in our own work. Enjoy these letters and embrace spirit.

Blessed Be

Angels

Dear Reader,

As long as humans have been walking on this planet, we have had spiritual beings that have walked beside us since the beginning of time. These beings show up in cave paintings, their faces etched on monuments and even in deserts in one form or another. They are spirit made whole. However they come about or whatever belief system you adhere to, no matter what time or culture, the spiritual beings of light - or angels - have walked beside us from infancy through our ages and will journey with us on to our next adventure of existence.

It may be difficult for some readers to understand, but though we are witches and work in the realm of magic and the Craft we do work with angels too. Angels are beings of spirit just as all humans are. Furthermore, spirit has no boundaries, colour lines, prejudices or preferences. Spirit simply just IS. No one religion has ownership of angels; if that were the case then you might as well say that the rainbow or the sunset belongs to you.

Angels can appear in many different forms though traditionally people depict them as human-like with flowing wings. However, they can also appear just as a being of light, a light as bright as the sun (though it does not hurt your eyes to look upon it). Angels can send us signs that they are around such as coins, flowers, feathers and other little signs that may be personal to you and that you would recognise, found in unusual places at significant times. That's what I love about angels, the personal touch!

In the last couple of years the idea of angels has become fashionable but for workers in the Craft and those who work with spirit, angels have always been 'in'. Many of us have in our homes an altar bearing symbols or ornaments of angels. This is for a number of reasons, such as to know that angels are physically around us at all times, to let others know that we work in light, or simply to show that we believe. They are a constant physical reminder of our faith and also to show the angels themselves how grateful we are to have them in our lives and that we welcome them into our homes and hearts.

If you would like to make an angel altar it is very simple. Just begin by collecting angelic statuettes. Look round the house as you may have some already. You may have angelic pictures on the wall. You may even have a pair of angel wings as an ornament. You will be surprised by what you may already have; the angels could have been in your life a lot longer than your conscious mind is aware.

Also on your altar keep the gifts that the angels leave you, like feathers or coins. For many years, wherever I would go I would find a two pence coin. Think about the symbols and signs that you always see or find. You could keep your communication with angels written in a separate book. Most of us write everything down in our Book of Shadows, but for angels you could create a separate book and call it your Book of Angel Shadows.

As for feathers, they do not always have to be white but can be various colours each with a different meaning. Generally the colours have the same meanings as with everything to do with magic. For example, green means healing or 'stop worrying about money'. But when it comes to finding feathers from angels it is a gift for you and you alone, so these following meanings are just examples and not absolute.

White	I will always be with you.
Grey, black	I know things are bad now but do not give up for I am with you.
Yellow	Well done, I am so proud of you.
Pink	Please love yourself as much I love you.
Red	Do not give in to anger over this problem. Take your time and do not rush.
Green	Do not fret over material things, all will be well and sorted.
Green, blue	I am sending you healing right now.
Purple	Please follow your heart as that is the way of spirit.

You could make a special angel candle. An explanation of and instructions for making various candles can be found in *The Craft in the City*. However, an angel candle is white with frankincense and spikenard oil in; if you do not want to make your own candle then anoint a bought one with these two very sacred oils. Afterwards, give thanks to the angels for helping you and for being there when you needed them the most.

Also on your altar you could have photographs of loved ones who are now in the spirit world, and have a piece of angelite or the simply beautiful angel opal. These are crystals that can be taken with you everywhere. You can recharge them on your altar in view of your candle light and then put them in your pocket[2]. Each piece of angel opal, or opal aura as it is otherwise known, is said to contain an angel! Enjoy this crystal as it is a very soothing stone. Keep it on your altar while taking the smaller angelite wherever you go. Further, on your altar do

---

[2] There is a full list of places to buy resources such as oils and special crystals in *Magic in the City*.

not forget to keep fresh flowers or a living plant; do not use artificial flowers as you want something that is living and real to honour angels.

Ouija Boards
As we are discussing angels, there is another aspect to this that needs to be explained - the ouija board, spirit board or angel board, which has suddenly become the fashion once again.

The latter part of the nineteenth century saw a rise in the popularity of spiritual séances. Table tapping became all the rage in Victorian society and was definitely a common part of an evening's entertainment. The early twentieth century did not discourage Spiritualism either; the two world wars become major factors in the quest for spiritual contact with those unfortunates who had passed over as a result. Yet out of this interest in Spiritualism came the ouija board (the name derived from both the French for yes, oui, and the German for yes, ja).

Traditionally, ouija boards were comprised of an oblong piece of wood with the alphabet printed in a semi-circular arrangement, together with a pointer (or upturned glass). Those participating would put a finger on the pointer and ask questions of the spirits. If you have dabbled with an ouija board you may have experienced the force with which the pointer will move from letter to letter. In the past, many Spiritualists would have used an ouija board to communicate with those who had passed away. Yet this was just part of those times, a part of the fashion and traditions dating back to the Victorian era.

My advice is that if a spirit wants to contact you they will. You do not need a board to contact them. If there is a message for you, they will find a way to tell you and they will tell you in a way they know you would understand. This is the same for spirit boards and angel boards, which are basically the same thing. If you need something like this to contact angels, one would have to ask what kind of spirit are you communicating with? Angels, spirits and spiritual guides do not need any form of equipment to contact you. Any being that works within the light and is a part of the light will leave you messages to let you know that they are around, such as feathers, coins, flowers and the scent of flowers, a warm feeling or an energy buzz.

If whatever you are trying to contact needs a board to come through, it is because its own door has been closed and it cannot wander freely as beings of the light do. Please do not use ouija boards. They can play with people's minds by tapping into the subconscious and the 'messages' may be upsetting and frightening. The beings of light do not do that, they do not frighten you and will only make their presence known if you are all right about seeing them.

Angels are wonderful beings of spirit to work with and we all have them around us. Get to know your angels and welcome them into your life.

Blessed Be

A Glossary of Angels

Here is a list of angels, some of whom you may know but some you may not. Our information about angels comes from a wide variety of sources and emphasises the many cultural influences in our belief systems. There is literally 'a host' of angels and some religions believe that each of us have a personal angel, which would run their number into billions.

Adnachiel The angel of November and the ruler of Sagittarius.

Ambriel The angel of Gemini.

Asmodel The angel of Taurus.

Barachiel The angel of February and responsible for Pisces.

Chamuel This is the angel who wrestled with Jacob.

Doniel One of seventy-two angels with dominion over the zodiac.

Emmanuel The angel of protection, whose name means 'God with us'.

Furmiel An angel of the eleventh hour of the day. (Eleven is a very mystical number - see *Magic in the City* for an explanation of numerology.)

Gabriel	His name means 'God is my strength'. Gabriel is one of the two highest ranking angels, second only to Michael.
Gambiel	The angel of Aquarius.
Hahaiah	This is an angel of the Cherubim order. He is an angel who influences thoughts.
Hamaliel	The angel of Virgo.
Haniel	The angel of Capricorn.
Itqal	The angel of affection.
Javan	A guardian angel, especially for Greece.
Kuriel	One of the twenty-eight angels who govern the mansions of the moon.
Loquel	An angel of the First Heaven, of which there are seven.
Malchedael	The angel of Aries.
Michael	He is ranked as the greatest of all angels.
Muriel	The angel of Cancer.
Nachiel	The angel of the sun. Nachiel has rulership of Leo and his cabbalistic number is 111.
Orion	Not only a constellation but also the guardian angel of St Peter.
Paschar	One of the seven guardians of the Veil of the Seventh Heaven.
Qafsiel	Angel of the moon and guardian of the Heavenly Hall.
Raphael	Angel of healing. He is often viewed as being one of the three great angels alongside Gabriel and Michael.

Sandalphon	The angel of glory. He is also regarded as the tallest angel.
Sartzeil	The angel of Scorpio.
Tsadkiel	The angel of justice.
Uriel	He is a leading angel and often regarded as 'the fire of God'.
Verchiel	Angel of the month of July and therefore ruler of Leo.
Weatha	Angel of the Seal.
Xathanael	The sixth angel created by God.
Yerachmiel	One of the seven angels who rule the Earth. The others are Uriel, Raphael, Raguel, Michael, Suriel and Gabriel.
Zuriel	The angel of Libra.

Axis Mundi

Dear Reader,

In the Axis Mundi we find spirit because it is the spiritual centre of the world. It is the place of connection between Heaven and Earth, the higher realms and the lower. In spirit we find our ancestors and others who have gone before us. Many countries and traditions have their own ways of honouring their ancestors. In Japan the burning of incense is a part of ancestor worship while in China people believe their ancestors live on in their homes. One of my favourite traditions is that of some Native American tribes who believe that the deceased have just moved a little way from the village, they are just sort of 'next door'. An Aboriginal ritual was to carve mythical animals into the bark of trees to honour the spirits of the ancestors.

It is by way of the Axis Mundi that we can pass from the Earthly plane into the spiritual plane. Therefore not only is it the cosmic centre that lies within everyone, it also exists everywhere at once. The Axis Mundi is literally the spirit.

The summer and winter solstices represent the Axis Mundi. Although our concept of time is different to that of spirit, by recognising solstices we are centralising and acknowledging the physical manifestation of spirit in our experience of time. You could have a piece of rhodozite in the spiritual centre of your home, on your altar. Rhodozite is powerful around the time of the solstices in both the northern and southern hemispheres. It is a crystal that draws power from the sun at midsummer and welcomes the return of the sun at midwinter.

The actual term Axis Mundi means sacred space and it is often depicted as a tree[3] although it can also be a mountain or a pillar. It is spirit connecting the Earth to Heaven. The Axis Mundi is the centralised spirit within. At times, those who pass through the Axis Mundi can find themselves lost on their way. We often call these beings ghosts or spirits and there are five categories of them.

Apparitions
These are the most common and traditional of ghosts. They are the shadowy figures that appear and then disappear. These are the ghosts that appear at historical buildings or haunt the cellars of pubs or old theatre houses. Apparitions can be anything from people to animals to ghost ships, objects that mysteriously appear and then disappear.

Hauntings
Hauntings can go on for years, whereas poltergeist activities (see below) are usually of a short duration. A haunting can have all of the above forms. Yet they can be triggered by a disturbance within the environment or the earth. In many houses where there are hauntings, there may be cold spots (and high energy bills!). Hauntings can be explained in many cases by an investigation into underground rivers and streams.

But in our world history, certain dramatic events can imprint themselves on the subconscious of the environment itself. Therefore, ghosts or spirits can become trapped in the fibres of time and their images eternally reactivated, which is what a haunting is. For example, the spirit of a murder victim is often said to return to the scene of their death as a

---

[3] See especially The Yggdrasil in *Magic in the City*.

vengeful reminder. If there has been destruction on a grand scale in the environment, it could quite possibly have left an imprint, an echo or vortex as we would call it. In the vortex there may be a number of hauntings or sightings of different occurrences happening quite regularly. For example, if you live in an environment which was bombed during the Blitz and you are encountering 'happenings', it might be worthwhile talking to your neighbours as they may be experiencing something too.

Influences
These are ghosts who manifest a 'feeling' in a place or occasionally in objects. They are unpleasant but do not form any tangible reality. You may also smell a terrible odour; when it comes to ghosts, if it smells bad then the spirit is not good while if the smell is sweet then so is the spirit. Spirits of children often bring in a sweet smell with them, and angels can also bring a sweet smell of flowers. In either case if you are not happy with the influence, bad or good, you can just ask them to leave!

Phantasms of the living
In the next letter we shall look at the doppelganger, which I believe many phantasms to be. Essentially, phantasms are apparitions of people who are still alive and who appear in one place while their physical body remains in another. These phenomena usually involve people who are on the point of crossing over and who manifest themselves to loved ones in order to bring a message. Phantasms can also be people who are astral projecting their spirit, either intentionally or spontaneously. Either way, the phantasms of the living can be explained as astral projection.

Poltergeists

The name literally means 'noisy ghost' due to the noises and disturbances they make; they really are a nuisance. They manifest themselves by destructive outbursts of energy that can cause physical objects to move around the house, crashing and banging. The poltergeist may also manifest itself by moving or levitating objects. Some believe that these phenomena are caused by the disturbed energy of living people in the vicinity.

Ghosts may be perceived in different ways. Some people may just feel or sense a presence but they can also be experienced by other sensory perceptions such as a changes in temperature, a movement, a touch, odours, and sounds such as voices, music, tapping, rapping or scratching on the walls. If the noise happens suddenly and is a nuisance then it is highly likely to be a poltergeist activity.

At times, 'something' may just stop by. You may feel a presence for a couple of weeks and then it goes. For whatever reason, some beings just pass through and in this case it is best just to leave them alone. However, if something lingers or begins to make a nuisance of itself, such as by moving objects or throwing things, then ask it to leave. Treat them as you would any other uninvited or unwanted guest. Be polite and ask them to leave. Never be afraid and if you need a little extra back up then ask your angels.

On the other hand, if you feel that you seem to be attracting a lot of 'guests' then this could be the spirit world telling you to work in this area as a potential medium. You could invest in a piece of spirit quartz, or cactus quartz as it is also known; this can act as a form of protection and welcomes good company. When buying a piece of spirit quartz, the more crystals growing on it the more powerful its energies, though even a small piece is very effective. Place it in the centre of your room where you feel the most 'vibrations' and ask that only energies that bring love and positivity are allowed into your home. The other crystal that is often used to help with seeing ghosts is called phantom quartz. It is sometimes looked through by spirit investigators in order to see a ghost or phantom. However, if spirits want to appear to you or show you anything, then believe me they will and you will not need a crystal to see them.

Above all, when working with or experiencing spirit, do not be afraid. The spirit does not do harm; it is only our own fears projecting pain and suffering that are negative manifestations of thought. You are a being of magic and of spirit. You have all the power you need. Have faith and believe in yourself.

Blessed Be

Doppelganger

Dear Reader,

It is said that we all have a double, someone who looks exactly like us. However, throughout the centuries many people have actually seen their double, or doppelganger as it is known (its literal translation is spirit double). One of the most famous stories concerning the doppelganger is that of Queen Elizabeth I. It is said that she saw her spirit double on her death bed. However, on this occasion we would say that what she actually saw was probably an astral projection of her own spirit preparing to leave and cross over.

There are many stories of people seeing their doppelganger and then dying, which led to the belief that after seeing one's double one would die within moments. The more likely explanation regarding these cases is, as above, that of astral projection and it is the person's own soul which is preparing to cross over. Somehow our consciousness has allowed our soul to be free and therefore what we are witnessing is our own death. We do not have to look very far to see the similar modern day accounts of out-of-body experiences (OBEs) and near death experiences (NDEs). People report these when in trauma rooms in hospitals or when they are very sick, those who clinically die for a number of minutes.

The experiences of doppelgangers that are witnessed by other people are more interesting. The story of a nineteenth century school teacher is very puzzling: the teacher was seen for a full year in the classroom with her pupils and in the school grounds at exactly the same time.

A doppelganger is said to appear as completely life size yet colourless and transparent. Even more telling is that sometimes it does not appear completely and it is just with a facial form. Therefore it could be argued that the doppelganger is not a separate entity that looks like you, it actually is you.

The ancient Greeks believed that seeing one's own double was an omen of death, though ancient belief also stated that we all go through life with a spirit friend who is identical to us, our spiritual twin. But the ancient Egyptians did not share these beliefs and had their own name for the doppelganger, the Ka, which has the same memories and feelings as the person's physical self. Even in today's technological society there are still people who report seeing a loved one's double just at the moment of their passing; however, in these cases it is actually that person coming to say goodbye. And of course witches were often accused of sending their souls in the form of a body double to do 'wicked errands'. This actually refers to astral projection, a technique described in *Magic in the City*.

I would argue that the doppelganger is not a harbinger of death or bad news, but indeed something we can use to see the future with. The spell of an unmarried girl or person to see their future spouse is centuries old: one is supposed to eat an apple on Hallowe'en and look into a mirror by candle light so as to see one's future spouse's doppelganger peering over one's shoulder.

To connect with one's spiritual self or soul twin is to open oneself up to the possibility of spirit. This may sound strange; while you may believe in spirit it is another thing entirely to connect with the spirit that is inside you in the physical world. If you want to connect with your doppelganger, or your spiritual twin, then firstly you could invest in twin quartz. This also goes by the name of the Gemini quartz for obvious reasons, as Gemini is the zodiac sign depicted as twins. Now perform this ritual, protecting yourself in a circle of magic salt before lighting two identical white candles and placing the twin quartz in between the candles. Allow yourself to go deeply into a meditative state and then call forth your spiritual self. Ask yourself to manifest in front of you. Ask yourself whether your spirit is happy or if there are any parts of your life you could change.

Working with our spiritual twin takes time and we must let the answers come, as the spirit will always be honest with us. So be prepared. Afterwards, give thanks to your spiritual twin and tell it to return within you. Then speak these words as your blow out the candles:

> *Spirit to spirit, I called to thee.*
> *Rising smoke, spirit return to me.*
> *Spirit to spirit, Blessed Be.*
> *An' it harm none, so mote it be.*

You might feel extremely tired after doing this ritual and I would suggest you do it once and then leave it a month or so before attempting it again. On the other hand you may actually be full of life, quite literally on a spiritual high as you have connected with a part of you that wanted to talk with you. It is not a harbinger of doom! It is not negative, it is you and you are divine.

It is worth attempting to connect with your spiritual twin but if you do not feel comfortable with this then do not participate in the ritual and merely light two white candles in honour of your twin. When it comes to spiritual things, only ever do what feel right to you. Trust your instincts as, at the end of the day, instinct is your spiritual guide and that is where your twin lives.

Blessed Be

Dragons

Dear Reader,

Dragons have been written about in every culture and society in the world. The earliest descriptions and writings of dragons can be seen as far back as the fourth millennium BC. Many people believe that the dragon myth stemmed from the discoveries of dinosaur remains by early man. Yet dragons feature in every culture - the Chinese even have one for their astrological year[4] - while the planet Venus was known as 'the fearful dragon', its clothes on fire, by the Assyrians.

The physical description of the dragon is almost identical to that of a lizard or a long snake with wings. They are generally larger than elephants and are regarded as having long fangs and twin horns. It is generally agreed that most dragons are covered in scales though there are some that have leathery skin. Their colours can also differ, anything from red to green, black and gold being the most common.

Dragons seem to have a bad press. They often appear as evil, village-burning, virgin-eating destroyers and harbingers of doom and gloom. Yet nothing could be further from the truth. Dragons are powerful, strong and at times self-sacrificing. The legend of the Four Dragons in China tells how these wonderful beings saved the people. The dragons noticed that the people were starving and dying of thirst as the Jade Emperor had not

---

[4] The twelve Chinese signs of the zodiac are the rat, ox, tiger, rabbit, dragon, snake, horse, goat, monkey, rooster, dog and pig.

allowed the rain to happen, so they unleashed the waters that were in the four great rivers of China, knowing that they would have to remain in the rivers for eternity. This is a beautiful story, one that shows the self-sacrifice of the dragons and tells how these rivers got their names due to the dragons' colours: the Black Dragon became the Heilongjiang in the far north, the Yellow Dragon became the Huanghe in central China, the Long Dragon became the Changjiong or Yangtze river in the south and the Pearl Dragon became the Zhejiang River, the Pearl River in the very far south.

Thus in China as in other cultures the dragons have power over water, rainfall, hurricanes and floods. But in all cultures the dragon is a symbol of power, strength and also good luck. It is accepted both in the west and the east that dragons are magical creatures of nature and have the ability to breathe fire, while some can even breathe frost, lightning or gas. Therefore, dragons can be a formidable enemy. Yet they are friends to humans. They have cared for us and they protect us. They are the embodiment of every element we work with - water, air, earth and fire; they swim, they fly, they are of the earth and they can breathe fire. If you have nothing else on your altar, the symbol of the dragon is perfect for precisely those reasons.

Dragons also care for and look after the Earth. We owe a lot to them and we are very similar to them. We are of the Earth, we have water in us, we have fire as passion and we are also of air, not only the air we breathe but also the air that is spirit or soul, the divine that can also be depicted as a flame. We are indeed very close to our brothers the dragons. There is something else on this planet that also contains all the four elements and that is salt. Salt is from the earth and also from the sea, it is dried by the air and when you put a small piece on your tongue it burns, so it is also fire. In *The Craft in the City*, salt and the making of magic salt is discussed in detail.

If you want to honour the dragon on your altar, have a small dish of magic salt or sea salt on it. The crystals you can have to connect with dragons are dragon stone and dragon eggs. Another wonderful crystal to have in honour of dragons is zincite, a great and powerful crystal of fire energies, perfect for performing ceremonies and rituals in which dragons are the guests of honour.

Dragons, of course, are not just symbols of power or fire. They are also the keepers of gold and wealth. Just as mermaids love shiny baubles then dragons love gold. If you would like to tap into this energy of wealth then cast the following spell.

Light a gold candle and say these words over it three times:

> *Brother dragon, hear my song.*
> *Let my finances do no wrong.*
> *Bring forth treasures of old.*
> *Let me always own gold.*
> *My brother dragon, Blessed Be.*
> *Thank you for what you do for me.*
> *An' it harm none, so mote it be.*

Put out some gold jewellery if you have some. If not, you might think about investing in some gold or, even better, have someone buy you gold for your birthday! Let the spirit of dragons into your home and feel protected by them. They truly are a wondrous part of spirit that we should not forget. Enjoy working with your dragon.

Blessed Be

Elves

Dear Reader,

In Iceland the belief in elves is so strong that there is a special school to learn about them. The school is called Alfaskolinn and it is based in Reykjavik, the capital. It teaches students about the hidden people and the thirteen different types of elves. In Iceland there are even special 'elf investigators' who make sure that potential new building will not disturb the elves; there are plenty of tales about jinxed buildings and cursed factories and homes because people ignored the warnings and disturbed the elves.

These little beings have been with humans since the beginnings of time. Many people believe in ghosts yet when we mention the elves people dismiss them. But if ghosts are manifestations of air within spirit then elves are manifestations of earth.

Scandinavia is steeped in tales of elves primarily due to the beliefs of Norse mythology. On the world tree, the Yggdrasil, there are said to be nine worlds; one of these is Midgard, which is Earth and is presided over by Thor, our protector. The fifth world is Alfar which is the land of the elves.

The elves are thought to be small supernatural beings and there are light elves and dark or black elves. The light elves are often regarded as tall and beautiful, semi-divine beings that are rather ambivalent towards humans, neither helping nor hindering us. They seem to be very similar to ghosts or spirits insofar as they can pass through doors and walls. They are ethereal beings, often depicted with blond hair and blue eyes.

The elves of the lower kingdom are the dark elves that live in caves and in the earth and the dark forests. They are often regarded as being much smaller in stature than their light cousins. To all intents and purposes the dark elves are very similar to what we call dwarves in our spirit lore.

Within this realm we can find gnomes who are also earth spirits. Gnomes live underground and cannot stand the sun; it is said that one ray of sunlight would turn them to stone. That is probably why we have so many garden gnomes! Instead, during the sunlight hours they spend their time as toads. Gnomes are also related to goblins and dwarves.

Throughout the centuries the elves began to get a bad press and anything mischievous has always been blamed on them (though normally there was a witch behind the elf prompting it in their deeds!). The terminology during the Middle Ages began to draw on the experiences people had around them and one of the delightful terms was 'elf shot', referring to someone who has been taken ill in a town or village as a result of a witch's spell. Thus the elves began to take on negative connotations. Another term is 'elf lock' for people who have a tangle or knot in their hair, as it was believed that elves came and tied people's hair up in knots at night. So people began to think of ways to stop these naughty elves and devised the 'elf cross', said to protect against malevolent elves; the elf cross is actually our pentagram, which was painted on doors and stables across Scandinavia.

Elves and dwarves feature in many cultures all over the world. The little people have walked this Earth as long as we have been here. In Central America there is the legend of the Red Dwarf who uses his axe to cause sparks so that a seer can interpret someone's fortune from them. In Native American cultures the dwarfs and elves appear in many of their myths and legends, usually associated with mountains and rivers, such as the Awakkule who are strong mountain dwelling dwarves.

Elves are distinct from other beings of spirit as they do not have wings and are very humanoid in appearance. The one thing they do like, however, is a good sing-song. Elves are renowned for their dances and can be seen dancing over meadows at night and on misty mornings. They leave behind what we call 'fairy rings', which are circles of mushrooms or bare patches of soil. So if you would like to get in touch with your elf, or the elves in general, then put on your favourite song and dance around the house. Imagine the elves joining you in a dance and say this spell as you do:

> *Dear elves, come join me in a dance.*
> *Let us do a jig and be merry.*
> *Please enjoy and if by chance*
> *You shall want to stay,*
> *You are more than welcome here,*
> *Both by night and day.*

To embrace the spirit of the elves is to embrace freedom. They are liberty and independence. We have so many constraints in our day to day lives; fully to embrace the spirit of the elves is simply to let go and we all need to do that at least once in a while. Embrace the freedom of the elves and go to a museum, the cinema or a gallery; the more you do so the stronger you will become and you will feel a strength within you that has always been there but you may never have explored. Spirit is about that. Spirit can give you strength. Spirit is always there.

Blessed Be

Fairies

Dear Reader,

There has been so much written about fairies that it seems little else could be said. However, what some new readers or practitioners may not know about them are the legends or what people used to believe about these little sprites in the past. Fairies are also known as 'the wee folk' or 'the good neighbours'. Though they may come in many forms, some people believed they are fallen angels or that they are the souls of unbaptised children. Others have unfairly regarded them as the heathen dead and therefore neither good enough for Heaven nor bad enough for Hell.

Yet nothing could be further from the truth. These last two examples of explanations for fairies are obviously from the Christian era (terms such as baptism and heathen are cultural indicators) but fairies pre-date Christianity. Indeed, most if not all of the elementals described in this book pre-date Christianity. These energies, or entities, have been around since the beginning of time and have walked with us throughout our history, their legends and stories passed down by oral story-telling. It was only in the Christian era that we began to write them down as more and more people became able to read and write.

Every culture in every part of the world has some form of fairy or elemental being. What they truly are, or what their real purpose is, only a chosen few mortals ever really know. Yet despite their varied shapes, sizes and colours, one thing about fairies that people agree on is that they are rather mischievous little beings. Fairies delight in leading curious mortals astray - maybe we deserve it. Fairies are beings of the elements of air, earth, fire and water, beings of nature; all we need do is look around and see what we have done with nature, and no wonder they lead us astray! Or have we led them astray?

Nevertheless all fairies have the power to bestow good or bad luck. Some might say that the fairy's natural tendency is to be rather wicked and spiteful; for example, even when a fairy grants a mortal three wishes there is always a catch! People use the example of Cinderella's fairy Godmother who made sure Cinders got to the ball alright but put in the clause that at midnight her coach would turn into a pumpkin and Cinders would be back in rags. And Tinkerbell made sure the lost boys shot Wendy because she was jealous of her. Further, let us not forget that in the Craft we give our new-borns a magical third name that only they can recognise, in case the fairies swap the child and leave a changeling in their place. So granted, fairies are not all the wonderful little beings of childhood and innocence.

Fairies are often regarded as having fabulous wealth and are also fiercely protective of their homes. Woe betide the human who violates a fairy hill; it is said that those who do will endure ill-fortune, ill-health, disaster and even death!

Fairy rings are bare patches of soil that appear in the garden after fairies have been dancing round in a circle. They are thought to be lucky. However you are advised not to step inside as the fairies might take revenge. If you are lucky enough to have a garden, you might like to use part of it to create a fairy garden and invite these little elementals of spirit into your home. The main plants to grow are lily of the valley and snowdrops, but fairies love the sweet sounds of nature so make sure bluebells are there too. Being rather contradictory little beings they may like a wild garden but at the same time they love order and will not go anywhere messy. So an 'ordered chaos' of a garden is perfect for them. A lawn of forget-me-nots or chamomile and daisies also provides good paths for those fairy feet to tread. Rosemary, thyme, lavender, primrose and winter pansies are great plants to keep in pots; sun catchers and sparkly things, flowers and plants that smell nice and things that make noises are all ideal in a fairy garden. If toadstools suddenly crop up in your garden, then you will know you have fairies there.

When creating a fairy garden, imagine you are making an environment that wildlife will feel at home in. Therefore it is a place in the summer that bees and butterflies will flock to and feed on all the bounteous nectar, while in winter it will be a place that hedgehogs and ladybirds might want to nest in and huddle down in during frosty mornings and freezing nights. And if you can, have a wishing well no matter how small in your garden as fairies love them and use them as portals or magical doors.

If you do not have a garden, just a patio or balcony, then use lots of containers to create your garden. Lots of plants do better in their own space anyway, like herbs such as mint, lemon balm and sage. As with everything in spirit and magic, work with the environment you have in creating what you desire. Even indoors you can grow many herbs and plants; one of the best for fairies is the violet with its small delicate flowers.

Plants for an all-year-round fairy garden

Spring

Primrose, daffodil, tulip, crocus, dahlia, geranium, petunia, clematis, wisteria and bluebell.

Summer

Bluebeard shrub, butterfly bush, smoke bush, foxgloves, oleander, rock rose, Potentilla, Spirea, rose of Sharon (particularly Minerva for obvious reasons) and Summer Sweet which has a lovely fragrance. Hydrangea Paniculata can be kept in a container. Carolina Allspice is also good but on no account must you eat it as this is not the cooking allspice from a completely different plant. Instead you can use the seeds for pot pourri or grind them up for incense.

Autumn

Aster, helianthus, honeysuckle, Penstemon, anemone, dahlia, Echinacea, phlox, socks, viola, hollyhock, helenium (particularly the one called Autumn Lollipop), poppy (Coral Reef is especially beautiful), and Corydalis Flexuosa China Blue which is simply gorgeous - it looks like a fairy waterfall of blue trumpets, and mixed with Corydalis Canary Feathers is a beautiful display of colour.

In autumn you could also start to prepare 'houses' for wildlife to survive the winter in. Keep a couple of empty flower pots on their side and put some dried leaves in for insects and wildlife to hibernate in during the winter. Hedgehogs curl up in a ball and hibernate for five months in a nest of grass, moss and leaves somewhere quiet where they will not be disturbed.

Winter

The cold and frosty mornings of winter are still magical. There are many plants that flower at this difficult time here in the northern hemisphere, and a winter flowering shrub adds a burst of colour to the landscape. Winter jasmine has trumpet-shaped flowers appearing first, followed by small glossy leaves. Here are some other flowers that the winter fairies will enjoy:

Snowdrop, Glory of the Snow which has star-shaped blue and white flowers, pasque flowers which are bell-shaped, crocus which comes in yellow, white and purple, winter squill which has green leaves appearing first followed by bluebell-like flowers, the Christmas Rose with white flowers that blooms in the middle of winter (for us it is a perfect flower for our Yule altar) and Viburnum Tinis - a bushy evergreen shrub with pointed oval leaves and heads that have pinkish white flowers with a sweet smell.

No fairy garden, or witch's garden for that matter, would be without winter aconites. They grow in sheltered spots in flower beds and under trees, their small yellow flowers making an appearance in late winter. Another plant for your garden is any tree that has catkins on it. Catkins come out in late winter or early spring before the leaves open.

If you plan it correctly, your fairy garden will be full of life and colour all year round. Remember to leave little gifts out for the fairy folk, even something like a needle and thread which comes in very useful for them. A crystal to have in your house or your garden is a piece of staurolite, as this is the fairy stone.

The fairies' colour is green as this is the colour of magic, nature and of the Earth that they look after. If you do happen to see fairies, never try to interfere with whatever they are doing. It is a mistake to try to control and imprison the fairy, for that is to destroy the very thing they love. Enjoy bringing the magic of fairies into your house and garden. It is a lovely friendship.

Blessed Be

The Lady of the Lake

Dear Reader,

The Lady of the Lake first makes an appearance in the legends and stories of King Arthur and Excalibur. This mysterious lady holds the sword Excalibur as the symbol of eternal power, magic and nobility. Hers is the watery world of magic and mystery. Just as the Lady of the Lake was the guardian of Excalibur, she was also revered as a Celtic goddess in some tales. However, for us the Lady of the Lake is regarded as one of the Ancient Ones, ageless and beautiful and immune to the effects of ageing and disease, beings who have been here long before humans, the keepers of ancient knowledge. They are neither angels, fairies nor gods.

The Lady of the Lake is neither a mermaid nor of the Merfolk family; she uses the lake and other sources of water as portals to other realms and dimensions. As one of the ancient wisdom keepers she has the ability to see the future. She knows the path that every mortal should and will take, and she will interfere by blocking someone's path with water of some kind to make sure they do take the right path. As an Ancient One, she is permitted to guide and influence us in some way. There are certain paths we must take at times. But equally we may come to a crossroads in our careers or in our relationships, or we may have many opportunities opening up to us, and at these times we simply do not know which path to take. It is then that we may call upon the help and knowledge of the Lady of the Lake.

If you can, try to buy an obsidian mirror. These have been used since ancient times and more recently by the Aztec civilisation and the English alchemist Dr John Dee. Obsidian mirrors are the perfect scrying resource. However, something even better is an obsidian bowl, so buy this if you are able to and if you intend to work a lot with the Lady. If not, any bowl with a dark base will be fine.

Fill your bowl with water and write out your questions concerning which path to take. Make sure you perform this ritual in a protected circle and have all the equipment already in the circle before you begin. Light one white and one blue candle. Take a couple of deep breaths and calm yourself, forgetting about the day and allowing yourself to receive insights. Begin to look into your bowl of water and say these words:

> *Lady of the Lake, I beseech,*
> *Show me what I cannot see.*
> *Unveil the mists of time and space,*
> *Show me the path I must take.*
> *An' it harm none, so mote it be.*

You are now scrying into a bowl of water. You may see images forming within the water or see the candle flames flicker. There may suddenly be a flash of an object in your mind's eye that you can relate the answer to. The questions we have are all individual and therefore how we receive the answers will also be individual and unique. You may see nothing when you cast this spell and yet you may dream the answer later on in the night. We must open ourselves to the possibilities.

Do not ask the Lady of the Lake for the winning lottery numbers as this is not appropriate. However, if your question is about a financial problem, numbers may appear; in this case then, yes, put them on your lottery ticket as you never know. If the Ancients have chosen to help you, my only advice is to go with it. If the Lady has chosen you as a pet, then be thankful and enjoy.

The Lady of the Lake is an ancient wisdom keeper of spirit. The information she knows and understands is unimaginable. She can also be called upon by having a piece of aquamarine in your pocket, or a piece of aqua aura. These stones are beautiful and very powerful, a connection to the Lady and a reminder that the ancients are always with us. Fill your obsidian bowl with water at a full moon and charge the crystals in it. If possible, place the bowl in view of the moon's rays saying these words:

> *Lady of the Lake I call to thee,*
> *Help me in my endeavours.*
> *Let these stones serve me well the whole month long,*
> *Help me to see the right from the wrong.*
> *Lady of the Lake, always be with me.*
> *An' it harm none, so mote it be.*

Do this ritual every month when there is a full moon as you are cleansing and recharging your crystal. In the morning, take the stones out of the bowl and leave them to dry naturally. Throw the water away, giving thanks for its healing, cleansing energies. With every use of your obsidian bowl, always tip the water away so that the bowl is dry for most of the time; it should only have water in it when you wish to use it for a ritual or for cleansing crystals.

Blessed Be

Leprechauns

Dear Reader,

Leprechauns are a part of spirit within the domain of the earth. They do not have wings and for all intents and purposes they are like small people. Their physical characteristics have been changed throughout the centuries to how we assume them to be and today we view leprechauns as simply male, dressed in green and sitting on toadstools. Yet this image is a modern day mixture of pixie, elf and fairy, while the original leprechaun was nothing of the kind.

It was in the eighth century that leprechauns began to make their first appearance in the tales of Ireland. This was at the time when people first began to write oral legends down yet the leprechauns, as with so many physical manifestations of spirit, have been with us for much longer. There are leprechaun women too and furthermore they do not sit on toadstools either for that matter.

What we do know about leprechauns is that they are native to Ireland, living in the hills and mountains there in a secret, sacred enchanted world that only they can find by the use of their shillelaghs. The shillelagh is a short, thick club that was carried as a defence against muggers and thieves. It is also known as a cudgel and is still very popular with people today for the same purpose. Many depictions of leprechauns show them with their shillelaghs and given that this was a weapon one can deduce that a leprechaun would defend himself at any cost.

Leprechauns are excellent makers of shoes. Further, one aspect that does transcend all the legends and stories about them is their love of gold. These curious little beings have particularly fabulous treasure hoards, whole pots of pure gold. To all intents and purposes the pot looks like a black cauldron, which only adds to the shine and glow of the gold.

Finding a leprechaun is tricky and catching one is even harder. However, if you do manage to find one the story goes that you must not take your eyes off the little fellow as he is likely to disappear and escape. You are then meant to keep him locked up until he tells you his secret of gold or grants you three wishes. However, always be careful when the wee folk offer you three wishes as there is likely to be a catch! Apart from making shoes, the leprechauns' task is to give out luck - which can be good or bad depending on what the recipient makes of it. Overall, though leprechauns might be tricksters they are certainly not evil.

There are many stories of leprechauns throughout Ireland, such as how they come down the mountains at night. Nearly every mountain or hill in Ireland has a story of the wee folk attached to it in some form. People have claimed to see little lights floating down the mountains; leprechauns are also renowned for stealing little dogs and using them as horses.

As leprechauns are fabulous makers of shoes, you could connect with them by sorting out all your shoes. This is a job for one of those rainy days, perfect Irish weather! Light a green candle, put on your favourite music and sort out all your shoes and boots. Clean and polish them and give away those you have not worn for years. If there are shoes that need mending and you still want to wear them then have them repaired.

If you have Wellington boots or shoes that are no longer worth wearing as they cannot be repaired, you could make them into plant pots. Spray them gold and put a trailing lobelia in them; this comes in a range of colours and is a lovely bedding plant for the summer that the elementals will appreciate. Leprechauns are spirit elementals with dominion over the Earth and that includes the plants and flowers. Ferns, lilies and flowers of golden yellow are the best ones to represent the wee folk of Ireland in your garden.

The crystals we use to acknowledge the leprechaun are of course goldstone and rainbow quartz for obvious reasons. However, another crystal that is perfect for this connection is Apache gold. This wonderful stone is a natural bringer of luck, something that the leprechauns can give to us mortals. Apache gold also helps to heal your finances and stops the flow of money draining away from us in difficult times. If you can obtain a piece of Apache gold, infuse it with the power of the leprechauns and ask for their support with your finances. Light a green candle and say over the stone:

> *Leprechauns, please hear my call,*
> *Timeless beings of Ireland's old.*
> *Bless this wondrous piece of gold,*
> *Grant upon it your leprechaun luck*
> *So that my finances cease to run amok.*
> *Thank you, leprechauns, and Blessed Be.*
> *An' it harm none, so mote it be.*

Leprechauns are a wonderful energy to connect with if they choose to work with you, though out of all the earth elementals of spirit they can be the hardest to work with!

Blessed Be

Merfolk

Dear Reader,

The one thing that about the Merfolk and mermaids in particular that cannot be denied is that they certainly know how to look after themselves. This can lead to some people calling them vain; yet we must all look after ourselves for if we do not then we cannot take care of others.

Merpeople, both mermaids and mermen, have been around for thousands of years and are recorded all over the world from Japan to Scandinavia, Babylonia and Mesopotamia. There are figures in ancient writings of men with a fish's tail and in the stories of the Arabian Nights there is the story of Abdullah the fisherman and Abdullah the merman. In Syria there are many stories of Merpeople and especially of a merman who had a human wife; the subsequent child, a son, of this couple spoke the language of both the land and of the sea. Now that's bilingual!

Closer to home, the British Isles are littered with stories of mermaids and mortals falling in love, from Cornwall to Scotland; indeed, one Scottish clan claims to be descended from a mermaid. The stories stemming from the British Isles regarding the Merfolk are endless but then again we are completely surrounded by water. Denmark is also a series of islands and let us not forget the most famous mermaid whose statue now graces the Copenhagen harbour. The North Sea and Atlantic Ocean around Scandinavia has its fair share of similar legends. These mysterious elementals of water are indeed magical.

The Greek islands have many legends of Merfolk, especially the Sirens who captivate fishermen and sailors with their song and lure them to their deaths on the rocks. Indeed, in ancient Greece many gods and goddesses came from the sea; the goddess of love, Aphrodite, came ashore in Cyprus as she arose from the sea foam.

The tales of mermaids in Ireland are countless. One of the many legends is that they were originally 'pagan women' who had been transformed into the shape of mermaids by Saint Patrick himself (the saint who was responsible for getting rid of all the other saints in Ireland). Of course, these pagan women could be called something else... witches! Indeed, Ireland has so many tales of Merpeople that they have their very own form of Merfolk, called Merrows, considered more gentle and beautiful than the average mermaid or merman. They have a fish lower torso like most Merpeople but the fingers on their hands are webbed. It is claimed that Merrows can announce the coming of a storm by a sighting of their presence. They are said to wear red feathered caps (whereas normal Merfolk do not have any caps), but if their caps are lost or stolen they cannot return to the sea as the caps help them to travel under water.

Another legend concerning mermaids is the one that stems from Biblical times, that Merfolk are Pharaoh's children who were drowned when Moses parted the Red Sea. The Merfolk of Japan are slightly more enchanting and alluring than some. The wonderful Ningyo of Japan is a water fairy who lives in a beautiful palace at the bottom of the ocean; when she cries, her tears are pearls.

The sea holds such mystery and power that it captivates us in awe. Merpeople are immortal beings who can spend an eternity at sea. On the whole, though, mermaids have more of a bad press than good. It is said that their hearts are as cold as the sea and oceans they swim in. However, there are times when a mermaid will fall in love with a mortal and she will come ashore, temporarily having legs and looking human.

The other beings of spirit with dominion over the seas are the Nixies. They are beautiful sea beings who look like living ice sculptures, though they can shape-shift and often appear as humans or beautiful white horses, which seem to be their favourite alternative character.

However, there is another being of the sea who is rather feared by all and that is the sea hag, or sea witch. She is often responsible for putting mermaids out of their torment when they have been scorned by a mortal, by taking their immortality so that the mermaid may die.

The legacy of the mermaid is taking care of oneself. She is all about you feeling good about you. If you want to connect with the spirit of the mermaids in general, then turn your bathroom into a spa, a watery domain of indulgence. The colours of the Merpeople are of course blues, whites and greens, the colours of the oceans. You could also try to make your own shower and bath products and your own soaps. You do not have to go to great expense as there are many kits available on the Internet that include the soap, essential oils for scents, colours and moulds at very reasonable prices. Your own 'mermaid basket' of handmade beauty products such as shell-shaped soaps, shower gels, bath salts, body scrubs and shampoos, complete with a mermaid candle, makes a lovely gift for friends and family. The mermaid candle and many examples how to make these products can be found in *Spells in the City* and *The Craft in the City*.

The stones and crystals we use to connect with the Merpeople are larimar, or the Stone of Atlantis, water sapphire, paua shell and of course pearls. Another lesser known stone for the connection to Merpeople is Neptunite, which is named after the Roman god of the sea, Neptune (though this stone is rather rare and very expensive).

The essential oils to use in candles and bath or shower products are sandalwood, eucalyptus, cherry blossom, vanilla, hyacinth and lilac. Light your mermaid candle and enjoy the wonder of water.

Above all learn to love yourself, which in this day and age is easier said than done. Yet think of the wonderful Merpeople and how free they are. Live for yourself at least for a little while and be free.

Blessed Be

Mothman

Dear Reader,

We find Mothman among all these ancient elementals as he too is a being of spirit from the past. Although people associate him with modern day experiences, the legends and stories of winged creatures go right back into our earliest recorded histories. From ancient Babylonia to ancient India where Hindu and Buddhist societies recorded a flying creature, all the way through the centuries to the Owlman of Cornwall and the Houston Batman of the modern era, the Mothman has appeared throughout time.

The one characteristic that seems to prevail with these winged creatures is that they are always precursors of disaster. The Mothman seems to be the prophet of doom who foretells death and destruction. But he does not create any tragedy or cause a catastrophic event to happen; if anything, these winged creatures seem to be warning us of some potential disaster.

One of the most fascinating modern cases of the Mothman happened in Point Pleasant in West Virginia in 1966, when over a thirteen month period more than one hundred people witnessed the Mothman. The main description of this being was that it looked like a man but with enormous wings and huge, fiery red eyes. The witnesses who saw this creature were, to say the least, absolutely petrified. Even after he had gone people still felt him, for Mothman had such a presence and left people with an eerie feeling. Those who saw him had no idea what he was trying to tell them.

However, thirteen months to the day after the first sighting of the Mothman, disaster struck this small town. The Silver Bridge collapsed on December 15th, 1967, and forty-six people were called to spirit. A lot of people lost loved ones and many people's lives were changed forever. The subsequent investigation found that a steel pin had caused the bridge to collapse. The number of the steel pin was thirteen!

The build-up of energy before something happens can often be felt all over the world without the need for Mothman to tell us. The birds stop singing when there is going to be a storm. One of our sayings is 'the calm before the storm'; we too can sense when something is going to happen, if only we would trust our instincts more.

The Silver Bridge collapse in 1967 was not the only recorded occurrence of the Mothman in the last century. People saw Mothman for several months in Chernobyl before the nuclear power plant failure of 1986, and people saw him leading up to the earthquakes in Mexico in 1985. At the turn of the previous century, people claimed to have seen a giant bird flying over Galveston in Texas and on the 8th September, 1900, a hurricane took away between six and eight thousand lives. This was the worst recorded hurricane disaster in the United States.

However, once again, these winged creatures are not the causes of disaster. The Mothman has often been compared to the Thunderbird of the Cherokee myth; the Cherokee believed that every twenty-seven years this giant birdman returns to Earth to steal away children. Yet whatever these winged beings are, they feature in many myths throughout the world. They are a consequence of the human condition.

Something else that is equally a fascinating part of the human condition is the phenomenon of crystal skulls, which can also be portents of doom. They tell us when something is going to happen. Crystal skulls are made from a solid piece of quartz, usually clear quartz. They are believed to be Mesoamerican in origin and are regarded as keepers of ancient knowledge. If you feel you have a connection to crystal skulls, then invest in a crystal skull tarot deck or oracle cards, of which there are many available.

You must follow spirit wherever it leads. However, I would advise caution concerning Mothmen - on no account attempt to contact them. Remember, they are beings of spirit that tell us of death and destruction. While they are not negative or evil, just another part of spirit that comes to us, we do not seek this one out. If we are fortunate (or unfortunate) enough to see Mothman, we should accept the experience and try to see what he is trying to tell us; but we must also listen to our own inner voice regarding the potential disaster and look for the signs. However do not be afraid. Never be afraid. No matter how foreboding some manifestation of spirit may be, you are spirit too.

Blessed Be

Nymphs

Dear Reader,

The lovely nymphs are a personification of nature. They are spirit manifested in nature itself. Nymphs are tree spirits who protect the forests, the woods and the eternal springs of life. They cherish and nurture nature and celebrate death as a renewal of life. Nymphs stem from Greek mythology and are regarded as semi-divine. You could call them the daughters of Gaia, for theirs is the Earth to protect and care for. They are indeed the natural florists of the world.

Nymphs are female spirits and are often depicted as beautiful young women who live in natural habitats, usually keeping to the forests and woods. There are many nymphs throughout the world who govern mountains, rivers and sacred springs, and there are specific wood and plant nymphs who may have different names such as the Meliae, the Dryads or the Naiads among many others.

They are always found in groups, usually of three but there can be more of them. As beings of divine origin and also beautiful young women, they have of course been pursued by countless gods such as Pan, Hermes and Dionysus. The nymphs who mated with Poseidon, the god of the sea, became mothers to their subsequent offspring. The rather formidable Cyclops is also the result of the union between a nymph and a god.

As nymphs are the personification of nature, they are also very much aware of the pleasures of the flesh. Sexuality is a part of nature, not just in the act of procreation but in the expression of love towards one another. Nymphs, of course, love to frolic and to be free; they are freedom-loving, wild and sensual beings who are well in tune with their own sexuality.

To enjoy and tune into this wonderful energy is to express your sensuality and to be confident with your own sexuality. The use of certain crystals and stones placed around the bedroom can enhance the pleasure and connection that comes with sex. One of the main stones for this is Shiva lingam. This stone unites and strengthens the sexual union between people. If you have been having problems with your partner, then this is the stone to place in your bedroom. It is also particularly good for fertility issues, so place one in your bedroom if you are trying to conceive. This stone is also beneficial for those who wish to practise sacred or tantric spiritual sex.

If the libido has been dwindling of late then another stone to use is red tiger's eye, or a ruby. Place these in the bedroom and see what happens. Another stone for creating a harmonious and long-lasting relationship that works well with the energy of the nymphs is moss agate. You can also use tree agate - its proper name is dendritic agate as it was named after tree in Greek. Tree agate is particularly good to use when we want to connect directly with the nymphs.

Sacred Sex Nymph Oil

If you would like to create your own massage oil that encapsulates the sensuality of the nymphs then try the following. Use almond oil as the base or carrier and mix with it 3 drops of cinnamon essential oil, 3 drops of ginger essential oil, and 3 drops of orange essential oil. Shake them together and keep the oil in a dark glass bottle, labelled and dated, in a drawer of your bedroom.

Nymph Love Oil

If you would like to create a different form of massage oil, one that ensures a strong and long-lasting, loving relationship, then try this. It is made the same way as above but instead with 3 drops of juniper essential oil, 3 drops of cedar wood essential oil and 3 drops of rosemary essential oil with a base oil of either grape seed or almond. Traditionally, for each massage oil you will need at least 30 ml of the base oil for a full body massage.

As you shake the bottle of massage oil, say this spell and as you do so imagine the night or day you want to have with your partner.

Miss nymph, bold and free,
Unite my love and me.
Let us be joined as two become one,
Let us have a night of love and fun.
Lady nymph, bless me with sensuality.
An' it harm none, so mote it be.

There is another thing that increases our sexual potency and that is an aphrodisiac. Early people did not necessarily know the chemical compounds that enhanced sexual potency or increased fertility, so many of the foods used became synonymous with both. Here is a brief list of some foods that have been considered as aphrodisiacs:

Almond, avocado, apple, aniseed, banana, cherry, chocolate, cloves, cinnamon, coriander, fennel, fig, ginger, ginseng, honey, mint (there was actually a beautiful nymph called Menthe), oyster, raspberry, strawberry, star anise and the humble tomato. However, in general all seed-bearing fruits are aphrodisiacs; their numerous seeds, texture and scent make them all rather sensual foods to eat - especially if dipped in melted chocolate!

The delightful nymphs are truly wonderful nature elementals of spirit. They express that part of us that most of us keep hidden in our day to day lives. Yet we should not be ashamed of our sexuality. When we meet the one we love we need to express our feelings in the most natural way of all. So embrace the freedom of the nymph and show your sensuality to those you love.

Blessed Be

Pegasus

Dear Reader,

The reason we find Pegasus in this book is simple. In the ancient world, any animal or being that is given wings has a connection with the spirit world either by virtue of being a messenger between Heaven and Earth (such as the Mothman) or because they are some form of deity. Wings themselves are symbols of knowledge and enlightenment (not to mention the freedom they can bring). The god Hermes has a wonderful pair of winged sandals and his job was as messenger of the gods; wings prove most useful especially when you are flying back and forwards between Heaven and Earth. And the most famous winged beings are the angels.

Nevertheless, the role of Pegasus is very special and unique for us. In many Greek tales, Pegasus is synonymous with bravery and adventure. He is often regarded as being divine, depicted as white in colour and the feathers on his wings also pure white. The colour white is of course another indicator of spirit. In this sense we can see Pegasus as a symbolic form of spiritual energy that allows him access to the gods and goddesses of Olympus (though not to the realm of the gods itself). Pegasus is forever immortalised in the heavens with the star constellation that is named after him. He looks down upon us every night.

Further, according to legends everywhere when Pegasus strikes his hoof on the earth a magical spring will burst forth.

He is symbolic of the energy of nature. He is also a friend to the Muses[5] and as such is a good energy to call upon in many spells for inspiration and knowledge, such as when we face exams or the writing of a dissertation or an essay.

Here is a spell for help with exams and for inspiration. Light a white candle and, if you can, have a white feather with you as you say these words:

> *Blessed Pegasus, mighty and strong,*
> *Let my answers be right not wrong.*
> *Give me inspiration in my answers,*
> *Let my dreams and creativity soar,*
> *Give me insight once more.*
> *Blessed Pegasus, so mote it be.*

The perfect stone to use with Pegasus energy is clear crystal quartz. This amazing crystal can be used for all purposes but particularly for expanding communication with angels and the universe, which is what Pegasus represents. Clear quartz is everything that Pegasus is and it can heal and re-energise the body.

Use the energy of Pegasus when you need to boost your output or you have an important exam or job interview. Pegasus embodies adventure and bravery so imagine him when you are confronted with a new idea and rise to the challenge, allowing Pegasus to take you there.

Blessed Be

---

[5] For a description of the Muses and their attributes, see *Magic in the City*.

Phoenix

Dear Reader,

As we have seen in previous sections regarding winged flying creatures, wings represent the spirit. Yet they can also represent divinity and nothing could be truer of the Phoenix. This magnificent bird should be in the realms of the divine and yet she chooses to remain here with humans on the Earth.

The lore of the Phoenix is that there can only ever be one Phoenix in the world at any one time. Each bird can survive nearly 1,500 years. If only she could tell us the history and secrets she knows!

During its lifetime it is said that the Phoenix never harms another living being, whether person or animal, and lives only on aromatic smoke for her main food source. Legend has it that she knows when the moment of her own death is nearing. It is believed that she flies to Phoenicia in Syria to find a date palm tree in which to build a nest. However, the nest is actually a funeral pyre; the Phoenix is consumed within the flames yet through the ashes is born anew.

This amazing bird represents the element of fire. As she is reborn from the flames, she represents so much for witches. Through her we can connect with sisters and brothers who passed into spirit in the fires of the dark times of persecution.

So the symbolic meanings of the Phoenix for us working within the Craft are threefold: she is unique, she is selfless and she is reborn from the flames. Yet despite her divine attributes there are similarities between her and the Mothman tales inasmuch as both can be likened to the Garuda bird of India or the Benu bird of ancient Egypt. Moreover, as we have seen in other letters the winged creatures of ancient times are also messengers. The message that the Phoenix gives us is one of regeneration, that from the depths of total annihilation we can raise again from the flames. We can be reborn into a new life.

A Spell for Rebirth
If you have been wronged or have been persecuted and someone has broken your trust, then tap into the energy of the Phoenix and be regenerated. Use a red candle to represent the fire from which the Phoenix is born. Use incense to represent the aromatic smoke on which the Phoenix feeds and say these words:

> *Let me be reborn, let me live anew,*
> *Let me see with new eyes,*
> *Let me nevermore look upon*
> *Those who wronged me with their lies.*
> *Let me be awakened to a new life of truth,*
> *Once more blessed with innocence and youth.*
> *Blessed Phoenix, so mote it be.*

Further, there is a fabulous stone you can use while working with the Phoenix bird for regeneration. The crystal to use is Falcon's Eye, sometimes called a Hawk's Eye stone. It is also a great stone for mind travel or remote viewing. Another great crystal which is relatively common is fire agate, or flame agate as it is sometimes called. Fire agate is perfect for connecting with the elementals of fire, of which the Phoenix is one.

Phoenix Incense
There is another thing that is good for using with the Phoenix. Incense is a wonderful resource; it represents so much

and costs hardly anything to buy or to make. If you would like to try making some Phoenix incense cones then try this recipe.

If you are going to make your own incense cones, then my advice is buy a specific pestle and mortar and use this only for incense making. Failing that, always thoroughly wash out your pestle and mortar but never use it for cooking. Always try to have your magical things separate from your cookery things - it keeps utensils and equipment special and sacred. Yet never go to great expense in buying different and special things; look round your house as you will probably already have many of the things you need.

To make incense, always grind and mix up the powdered herbs in a pestle and mortar as it makes the ingredients smooth and evenly distributes them. The second important thing about making incense cones is not to be tempted to make big ones. When it comes to incense, less is more; so always make small cones as they burn better.

1 tsp dragon's blood
1 tsp frankincense
1 tsp myrrh
1 tsp gum arabic
1 tsp saltpetre

Combine all the ingredients in your pestle and mortar and grind them until they are smooth and mixed together. The secret with incense is how much water you use. So I suggest using a pipette and putting one drop of very warm water in at each grind. Therefore you can see how the incense is binding together. Keep putting in a drop of water until the mixture resembles play dough. Then take a small piece out and begin to make the cone, rolling the mixture between your thumbs and fingers. Do not worry if it does not look perfect to begin with as practice makes perfect and you will get better. (You could always try practising with actual play dough or Blu-Tack to create the cone.)

Then place the cones on a sheet of wax paper and leave them to dry. After a day, move them around a bit so they are not staying in one place, as they can and will go mouldy. Continue to turn them round every day for three or four days. After this they should be dry enough to burn or store in your 'magic cupboard' until needed. You could put them in an airtight container with a label to say what type of incense they are, or keep them in a little organza bag of the corresponding colour for their purpose. For example, a green bag for the good luck incense for money, career luck etcetera, while a red one is for the Phoenix incense.

You could also make sage sticks, or smudge sticks, which are very easy to make especially if you have a garden and grow your own herbs. Sage is the main herb for all smudge sticks. The magic of sage is covered in *Magic in the City*. There are other herbs you can put with sage to create a specific smudge stick for your particular focus, such as healing, money, love and so on. Here are some examples:

Sage and valerian	Relaxation, calming and also to induce a peaceful night's sleep
Sage and honeysuckle	Love
Sage and mint	Money
Sage and rosemary	Healing
Sage and oregano	Family
Sage alone	Always cleansing and protecting

It is up to you what you would like to use, but when you start to make incense always keep a record of your recipes and ingredients in your Book of Shadows. It is so easy to forget ingredients and quantities, especially if you really like making incense because the possibilities are endless. You could make an incense for each of the elementals featured in this book or for the elementals of spirit that are personal for you.

Embrace the Phoenix, for no matter how bad things are we can rise from the ashes and live again for another day.

Blessed Be

Pixies

Dear Reader,

The pixie is a strange one to describe as he or she is neither fairy nor elf, but a strange mixture of the two. One thing that can be said of the pixies for certain is that they are connected to the Celtic and Pict people of the British Isles. Wherever there is a descendent of the peoples of the British Isles we are likely to find a pixie.

The pixie's appearance can differ from county to county in the British Isles but generally they all have pointy ears and translucent wings which are usually unseen. The do love to skip and run and jump and of course fly. Pixies also have a wicked sense of humour and love to play tricks on people, especially lazy people. So if you are having a 'duvet day' or couch potato day and suddenly feel little pinches on you it is likely to be a pixie prodding you to get a move on.

The Celtic pixies are often said to have red hair and to wear green. However, this seems to be one of those confusions we see through history and the descriptions of the sprites of spirit, as having red hair and dressed in green also matches the descriptions of the leprechaun. But the leprechaun is much bigger than the pixie (though she is in turn bigger than a fairy).

One exception to the rule is the English pixie Robin Goodfellow who is said to be rather tall. His appearance is such that if you met him you would certainly remember it. He is said to have purple eyes, white hair and rather long, pointy ears.

Robin Goodfellow has many names and we may also know him by his other famous name, Puck. Puck is a powerful trickster and not to be taken lightly. Further, he has astonishing shape-shifting powers. However, a particular characteristic of Robin Goodfellow is that he adores clothes and will trade services for clothes, always worth remembering if you meet him. You would know him anywhere - or would you? Remember, Robin Goodfellow has amazing shape-shifting abilities and can and will transform himself into anyone or anything.

Also in the realm of the pixie we can find hobgoblins, brownies and lobs, although the appearance of these little sprites is rather strange (it is said that the brownie has no nose). They are actually wonderful little friends to have around as they love to tidy and clean the house and they repay kindness by helping with household chores. In contrast, bad deeds can attract hobgoblins, brownies and lobs that are messy and will throw things round your house! They have also been known to steal horses and ride round on them.

If you want to get rid of a pixie, hobgoblin or brownie, then you have to give them a piece of clothing or a name. Think of the story of Rumpelstiltskin who, after the princess had found out his real name, held no more power or right over her.

It is this aspect of the pixies - that they love clothes and are busy, tidy people - that we can develop and contact them with. If you would like to work with pixie energy, then tidy and clear out your wardrobe. Remember, they love clothes so you could create a special little drawer for the pixie in case one makes itself known to you. If you are limited for space then you could sort out your clothes for summer and winter, for example, and keep some of them elsewhere (such as under the bed or at the bottom of the wardrobe).

As the pixie is both of the air and the earth within spirit, there are a number of stones that you can use to harness their energy. One of the best pixie stones is fuchsite, which actually leaves green and gold flecks if rubbed, resembling pixie dust. It is a lovely stone that brings harmony to the home so you could leave a small piece in your wardrobe, if it keeps getting messy, to bring the balance and tidiness that pixies like. Another stone you could use is ruby in fuchsite, which is perfect for nature spirits and also for those seeking love. And another crystal good for working with pixies is green aventurine; this stone is very popular and still relatively cheap to buy.

Pixies love a flower garden. They will like the flowers of the fairy garden but especially vibrant colours. The foxglove and the toadstool are particularly sacred to the pixie. So if you are lucky enough to have a garden, make sure you have these two plants and you will surely invite pixies into the garden, especially if you have a couple of pieces of fuchsite and aventurine around too.

The pixie is a lovely energy to work with and one that is always youthful, no matter how old the pixie actually is (which is considerably older than any living being). Enjoy working with them and invite the pixie home. Enjoy the playtime and fun of spirit.

Blessed Be

Salamanders

Dear Reader,

The salamander is a true elemental of fire within spirit. The belief that led many people to this thinking comes from the fact that salamanders like to nest in rotting logs. Therefore, when unsuspecting mortals threw the log onto the fire, the salamander would jump out in the flames. So people began to believe that they actually came from the flames and therefore were elementals of fire.

Salamanders - or newts as they are also sometimes called - are little lizard-like creatures that are amphibian. They are regarded as extremely lucky, so if you have one in your house or garden never frighten him away.

Salamanders represent a number of things and not surprisingly one of these is volcanoes. The salamander is also responsible for St Elmo's fire. This is the weather phenomenon that occurs during thunderstorms, a dancing blue-green-violet flame that can be seen above the masts of tall ships. Sailors always thought it to be an omen about the voyage.

However, they have a double meaning when it comes to love. On one hand they can be a symbol for chastity, virginity and loyalty. But on the other they are, after all, the elemental of fire and as such represent the flames of passion and all that is connected to it such as temptation and burning desire.

The stones or crystals to use while connecting with the salamander are numerous. There is of course the pumice stone, which is formed from the lava that spews forth from the volcano; this is relatively common and still quite cheap to buy. Another stone that is more expensive and becoming rare is vesuvianite. The vesuvianite stone is a lovely green colour and is used to dispel negativity. This stone is found around the volcano Vesuvius in south-west Italy, the temperamental volcano that took out Pompeii. Its last major eruption was in March, 1944, and it has stayed rather quiet since then…

Another way to use the energy of the salamander is for relationships of love, especially for passion and desire. You could create a special salamander candle, which is red with two drops each of ginger and cinnamon essential oil. Light the candle and focus on the night you want with your partner. Then say these words as you imagine and visualise the night:

> *Blessed little salamander,*
> *Let tonight be full of passion,*
> *Let my desire be filled.*
> *An' it harm none, so mote it be.*

If the night seems to be a little dull or is not going the way you wanted, then quickly say this spell further on into the night:

> *Fire light, fire bright,*
> *Salamander passion*
> *Be with me tonight.*
> *So mote it be.*
> *So mote it right.*

The salamander is also an excellent guest in ceremonial magic and many witches and wizards invite them into their ritual as the salamander represents the elements and is a lovely little fire energy to work with.

Yet with any energy of spirit you work with, always be grateful and always make sure that you close your rituals properly and do not leave any spiritual doors open. To close spiritual doors, always visualise yourself completely shutting the doors of the four elements and especially also the door of spirit, even putting a lock on the door and sealing it. Then spray your holy water around the room and house or sprinkle salt near the doorways. Magic and spirit is predominantly in the realm of visualisation.

Blessed Be

Serpents

Dear Reader,

In all of spirit no elemental has had more of a bad press than the serpent. Yet it was not always like this and in many cultures the serpent, or snake, is revered. Somehow in our western world the serpent is thought of as being evil, perhaps primarily due to misleading Eve in the Garden of Eden (and look how that ended for Adam and Eve). All throughout the western world, and especially where Christianity is followed, the snake is regarded as evil. It is said that the snakes of Ireland were driven out by St Patrick himself.

In every culture, in every part of the world, there is a story, myth or legend of some kind about a snake. In the Sioux tales there is the story of the young married woman called Onwi-Menocha who ran away with her lover the Great Serpent. Onwi-Menocha means 'woman of the moon' and she would run away into the forest to be with her lover where together they would perform the Dance of the Secret Loves.

Here in the British Isles the serpent is often associated with Cerunnos. The image of the ram-horned snake can be found everywhere and represents prosperity and fertility. Another famous tale about the snake or serpent is the story of Thor and the Midgard Serpent. In Norse mythology, Midgard is the Earth and the serpent is so big that he surrounds the Earth tightly. The legend says that when the world serpent lets go, the Earth or Midgard will end. Thor fights the serpent on a number of occasions but each time the serpent gets away. The final battle is one in which Thor does eventually win but at the cost of his own life, as during the battle he is bitten by the serpent whose venom kills him.

The aboriginal people of Australia tell the story of the Rainbow Serpent, while Hinduism, Sumeria, ancient Greece, ancient Egypt and China all have gods and goddesses who are serpents or half-serpent. In Buddhism, a great cobra covers Buddha so that the rain does not fall upon him while he is in a state of meditation.

The serpent in its truest form is often associated with healing and medicine. The international symbol of medicine is that of the rod of Asclepius, the god of medicine, which has a snake wrapped around his staff. The symbol is called the Star of Life and is blue and white. This is the positive image of the serpent, its ability to heal, to rejuvenate and to transform. It sheds its skin to begin again. Though not quite as endearing as the Phoenix, the serpent is a creature of transformation and survival, of healing and rebirth.

Yet so many people fear the snake. (The term for this is ophidiophobia, from the Greek 'ophis' referring to serpents.) Perhaps the negative view and fear of the snake comes from the fact that they like dark places and regularly hide under dark crevices and rocks. This is why the serpent is also the symbol of the underworld.

There are so many ways in which we can use the image and energy of the serpent. For us working in the Craft, the serpent can be used for healing, fertility, transformation, justice and protection. The serpent is a guardian and a protector for many things, especially something sacred.

Your home is a sacred place. It is your special place where you can rest, heal, transform, enjoy and be with loved ones. So we will use the energy of the serpent to protect and guard our homes. If you can, make a blue and yellow candle by pouring the blue wax in first and then allowing it to set before pouring yellow wax into your mould. Put two drops of eucalyptus essential oil in the blue wax and two drops of cypress oil in the yellow wax. If you cannot make your own candle, then anoint blue and yellow candles with these oils.

Find a picture or statue of a serpent and put this on your altar along with your candle. Light the candle when you are ready and say these words:

> *Guardian serpent, bless my home,*
> *Guard it always wherever I roam.*
> *Guardian serpent, Blessed Be.*
> *An' it harm none, so mote it be.*

In the ancient world, the snake had many uses and powers. At Delphi, which was regarded as the centre of the world, the Oracle or appointed priestess was also called the Pythoness after the legendary snake that had once guarded the shrine. The Pythoness has serpents around her when she delivered her messages from the gods, usually warnings, promises or prophecies.

If you would like to receive messages from spirit then the best way in this modern high-tech world is simply to dream them. (A full description of dream interpretation and symbols can be found in *Magic in the City*.) Interestingly, one of the oldest interpretations of a dream stems from Ancient Egypt and it is about a snake: 'If a man sees himself looking at a snake, then this is a good sign of abundance and wealth.'

Before you go to sleep, say this spell over and over again until you fall asleep. If you have a particular question about love, career, health or anything else, then think of that also while saying this spell:

> *Oracle, Oracle, send me a sign.*
> *Tell me the future for this life of mine.*
> *Oracle, Oracle, Blessed Be.*
> *An' it harm none, so mote it be.*

Further there is an excellent stone that is perfect for connecting with the serpent, the snakeskin agate. You could keep a piece by the door of your house for protection.

The serpent is an aspect of spirit that should not be feared. In the Craft, every animal and every creature is sacred, not evil. In the Craft there is no evil as some might believe. If people are frightened of snakes, it might be worth their while to question why this is so; it may be something from childhood or it could mean something entirely different such as a past life memory that is now impinging on life in the present. Embrace all within spirit and never be afraid.

Blessed Be

Sphinx

Dear Reader,

There is something so mysterious about the sphinx that seems to echo deep within us. If you have ever had the opportunity to see them in Egypt or in museums, there is a wonder to them that penetrates deep within our souls. Gazing upon their faces we seem to see secrets and mysteries unfolding within the Earth's events. The sphinx could be the keepers of the Akashic records, the history of the world from the past to the present and future.

Yet looking closer at these magnificent creatures there emerge two distinct forms, one masculine while the other is feminine. The distinction may explain more about the societies that created them than the actual sphinx itself. The sphinx of ancient Egypt is male while the sphinx of ancient Greece is female. Furthermore, not only are the genders different but so is the actual image of the sphinx. Generally, the sphinx has the head of a human, whether man or woman, but it has the body of a lion. The ancient Egyptian sphinx does not have wings, while the ancient Greek and Assyrian ones do have wings. Remember what was written in previous letters about winged creatures of the ancient world being divine. This is exactly how the ancient Greeks and Assyrians viewed their sphinx, as being divine in origin.

'The riddle of the sphinx' was a challenge that many young travellers and warriors had to face, as the sphinx guards the

Sphinx

Dear Reader,

There is something so mysterious about the sphinx that seems to echo deep within us. If you have ever had the opportunity to see them in Egypt or in museums, there is a wonder to them that penetrates deep within our souls. Gazing upon their faces we seem to see secrets and mysteries unfolding within the Earth's events. The sphinx could be the keepers of the Akashic records, the history of the world from the past to the present and future.

Yet looking closer at these magnificent creatures there emerge two distinct forms, one masculine while the other is feminine. The distinction may explain more about the societies that created them than the actual sphinx itself. The sphinx of ancient Egypt is male while the sphinx of ancient Greece is female. Furthermore, not only are the genders different but so is the actual image of the sphinx. Generally, the sphinx has the head of a human, whether man or woman, but it has the body of a lion. The ancient Egyptian sphinx does not have wings, while the ancient Greek and Assyrian ones do have wings. Remember what was written in previous letters about winged creatures of the ancient world being divine. This is exactly how the ancient Greeks and Assyrians viewed their sphinx, as being divine in origin.

'The riddle of the sphinx' was a challenge that many young travellers and warriors had to face, as the sphinx guards the doors to the knowledge of spirit. However, in Greek legends the sphinx is an evil monster that can destroy those who offend her. Therefore for us working in the Craft, the sphinx represents the mystery and secrets of spirit, the unknown that is hidden within all of us.

As a result, the sphinx is useful for helping us with spells to overcome mystery and secrets. If you feel mystery is around you either at work or in your love life, then call upon the power of the sphinx to help the truth come into the light. Light a gold candle and keep it burning as long as possible until extinguishing it properly - never leave a candle burning unattended.

Depending on which culture of history you feel called to, either the ancient Egyptian sphinx which is male and has no wings, or the female winged sphinx of ancient Greece, imagine your sphinx standing before you as you say these words:

> *Mighty sphinx, proud and strong,*
> *Truth and justice I seek.*
> *Help me confront those who have done me wrong.*
> *Let the secrets come into the light,*
> *Let your strength put things right.*
> *Blessed sphinx, an' it harm none,*
> *So mote it be.*

Furthermore, if you feel connected to the ancient Egyptian era and the deities of Egypt, then there is a stone that is perfect for you to use with your Egyptian sphinx, the Isis quartz. Isis is regarded as the Great Mother of All and her sacred number is five, a very good number for those working in the Craft. The crystal has five sides and is very appropriate for anyone who has experienced any form of abuse; combined with the energy of the sphinx, the self-healing and protection of these two is very comforting. It is also a lovely crystal to give to someone who has lost or is estranged from their mother.

However, if you are not drawn to Egypt then another stone you can use is the magnificent all-rounder that is tiger's eye. There are three kinds of tiger's eye, black, brown and red. When using this stone while connecting with the energy of the sphinx, a red tiger's eye is best, though any tiger's eye is good for connecting with the sphinx.

The sphinx is a powerful energy to work with, so always be thankful and express your gratitude after working with them.

Blessed Be

Unicorns

Dear Reader,

Much has been written about these wonderful beings and as such unicorns are the ultimate symbol of good magic for, just like the Pegasus, the unicorn embodies spirit. Unicorns are sometimes depicted as having wings, yet many medieval writings and art works depict them without. Instead, they look for all intents and purposes like white horses, goats or ponies with one singular horn protruding from their head between their ears. They do look very regal and honourable beings, so no wonder that many of the noble and aristocratic houses throughout Europe used their image as part of their emblems and coats of arms.

These majestic beings have often been revered and regarded as a friend to humans. We can find many references to them in the Bible; it is claimed that the unicorn was the first animal to be named by Adam in the Garden of Eden. Further, while we have the serpent considered as the embodiment of evil in the Garden, the unicorn represents the polar opposite. It is the unicorn who often acts as an intermediary between humans and Heaven, although some claim that the unicorn took the side of man in the fall from grace and departed the Garden with Adam and Eve. It is interesting that we still know the serpent, but where is the unicorn? He is lost to myth and legend within the pages of time.

The unicorn has now developed for us into a being that is still a friend to man and woman. We have images of them and we gaze at their pictures knowing that they represent magic. They are an unattainable form of spirit like air or gravity - we know it is there but we cannot touch it or feel it. In the Craft, we use the power of unicorns to perform healing.

There are a number of stones and crystals to use when working with the energy of the unicorn. Botswana agate is a wonderful stone for balancing your aura and your spiritual energies. It is a lovely blessing stone, as is blue celestite. Although blue celestite is associated with angels and communication with guardian angels, it is also perfect for healing and for contact with unicorns.

The unicorn symbolises the spirit in its purest form. The spirit within grows all the time without us knowing. At times, spiritual growth waxes and wanes like the moon, but it is always changing and always moving in some form. With every life experience, whether happy or sad, our spirit grows that bit more until at last our final journey when we become one with spirit in our final breath. The unicorn symbolises this spiritual growth. There is a wonderful stone to use for acknowledging spiritual growth, called the metamorphosis quartz. If you can find one with a star or patch of light inside it, so much the better. Metamorphosis quartz is said to contain its own guardian angel which can be contacted through the crystal.

Perhaps you have had a difficult time and feel as though you have come through the darkness. It may feel like you have come through a dark tunnel and are now venturing into the light. You may want to give thanks to spirit. Use the energy of the unicorn to do this.

Make either a blue or white candle with two drops of apple blossom essential oil, two drops of cherry blossom essential oil, two drops of orange essential oil and two drops of peach flower essential oil in it. Alternatively, anoint a bought candle with these oils. Place your metamorphosis quartz on your altar and light your candle. Give thanks to spirit and to the unicorns for their constant guidance and love in bringing you home. Here is a blessing you may choose to use:

> *Blessing to spirit, blessing to unicorns,*
> *Thank you for your guidance.*
> *Future, present and past,*
> *I am one with spirit at last.*
> *Your love has brought me home,*
> *I have come through the dark*
> *And walk among the light.*
> *Thank you spirit, thank you unicorns*
> *For your love, strength and might.*
> *Blessed Be to all.*

The energy of the unicorn can also be wonderful for focusing healing, as unicorns are perfect for healing work either for loved ones who are unwell or generally for 'whole world' healing. Draw down their power and energy for the healing of the world and to bring peace in places of conflict.

Using your blue candle and, if you can find one, a piece of healer's gold. This really is a wonderful stone for those who practise healing on a professional basis such as doctors and nurses, or for witches when we have healing as part of our rituals. It is relatively rare but look online to see if you can obtain a piece. Failing that, a nice piece of amethyst will always be just as good as this crystal is an all-rounder and can be used for anything and everything.

Place your healer's gold or amethyst on your altar and light your blue candle. Focus your energy on who is sick or on the world, such as for a particular situation or conflict. Imagine the energy and glow of the candle as a swirling light that spreads throughout the world to that conflict or sick person, healing them with its warmth. This is a healing visualisation and is perfect for when you cannot be there physically with the person. We send our healing thoughts and prayers to the sick and injured with the help of the healing power of the unicorn.

Unicorns are truly magical beings and an absolute pleasure to work with. If you are interested in unicorns and have a special affinity with them, there could be a message for you. If of all the magical beings of spirit that we have discussed, the unicorn is the one who calls to you the most, then perhaps you are a healer. You could be a healer of people or of animals, or a healer of the Earth working in conservation. As the world waxes and wanes too under its own spiritual growth, healers are needed more than ever. Thank you for your work.

Blessed Be

Vampires

Dear Reader,

It might seem odd to have the next two letters describing vampires and werewolves, but not all manifestations of spirit are light and fluffy like fairies and unicorns. There are in spirit elements that are transitional, timeless and foreboding. We are dealing with the unseen element that is spirit. Do vampires exist? Well, yes, but perhaps not in the context you think they do.

There has been so much written about vampires that it is hard to distinguish fact from fiction. The myth that all vampires stem from Transylvania is precisely that, a complete myth. As far as the locals believe, Count Dracula was not a vampire but a fictional character of the nineteenth century who has helped with tourism! There was a Vlad Dracul, but he was far from being the leader of the undead.

All manner of things exist that we do not see, such as air, gravity or electricity. We can see the effects of them, and we feel them, but we cannot see them. The same can be said of vampires. We know for a fact that there are witches in the world, yet witches are not green with hooked noses and riding broomsticks to get to work (though it would certainly make the commute more interesting). But seriously, all manner of things exist that we just do not see - or maybe we do not want to see them.

Think about your experiences in life with people - those that you are friends with or colleagues at work or even family members. Are there people you know who deliberately try to 'wind you up', or people who will deliberately get 'into your face' to create a reaction from you, albeit a very negative one? To put it simply, these are vampires. And that feeling when you have been in a meeting with someone and you leave feeling absolutely drained and exhausted... these are both cases of psychic attack, a vampiric psychic attack. They are people who basically feed off your life energy, who literally just drain you.

Compare this with when you come into contact with an Earth angel who leaves you with a happy, energetic and buzzing feeling. These people just bring a smile to your face and literally 'light up the room' the minute they walk in. There are people whom you meet and you even find yourself saying "They're not from here!" You are probably right. Earth angels are in complete contrast to the vampire.

Many psychic vampires live in cities as they feed on all the excessive energy that buzzes around cities. People who get attacked by psychic vampires may suddenly feel a pounding headache, a complete physical drain or have 'psychic tummy', which people think is a sudden attack of food poisoning or violent diarrhoea. After the initial attack you will resume back to normal, but during those hours after the initial attack you are quite literally drained. Further, it can happen to anyone, even seventh generation witches!

So be careful when out in cities or at concerts and shopping centres, as they can be found where there are lots of people. Think about the people you know who create a reaction from you. Think about meetings that seem absolutely to drain you. Vampires do not have long capes and only come out at night, neither do they haunt empty houses and churchyards; they can look like anyone and be anyone. The worst kind of psychic vampire, however, is the one who does not realise what they are.

Throughout history there have been psychic vampires. It has been claimed that Rasputin was a psychic vampire because of the hold he had over the Russian royal family. Further, how interesting that it was the young Tsarevich Alexis who had haemophilia, a condition in which the patient can bleed continuously and that Rasputin was alleged to have cured.

Yet vampires have been around for much longer than the nineteenth century. Some of the oldest tales come from China, India and ancient Babylon and vampires exist in at least ninety per cent of the world's beliefs and cultures in one form or another. In China, the Jiangshi is a vampire (sometimes thought of as a zombie) who can kill. Interestingly, in the myths concerned with the Jiangshi it is said that a mirror can get rid of him, or the wood of a peach tree or rice can disperse him. A bowl of rice spilled on the floor, apparently, will stop him in his tracks as the Jiangshi has to stop and count all the rice grains. This is very similar to our demon sticks, which are glass sticks that are full of beads and usually left by the door. The demon apparently stops in his tracks to count them, giving the victim the chance to flee the scene and come back with help. Mirrors are excellent magical tools and a full description of their magical uses can be found in *Magic in the City*. There are vampire cases all over the world and there continue to be even now; in December, 2012, people in a village in Serbia were living in fear as a number of strange such attacks occurred.

There have always been and will continue to be parasitic people who live off others. Unfortunately there is actually very little you can do to prevent a vampiric attack and eating huge amounts of garlic will not work! However there are some crystals that can prevent psychic attack. Red jasper is a perfect one to use for potential 'psi vamps', especially as it's red which of course is symbolic of blood (though the majority of vampires today, of whatever variety, do not drink blood. Blood-letting rituals were often used in the past in many cultures and belief systems as blood is the life force of a living human being or animal. Though animal sacrifice is still used today in many cultures, vampires feed on the life force of others but do not necessarily drink blood). There are a number of other stones you can use to rid yourself of a psi vamp, or to help with healing after an attack, such as bloodstone or blood agate.

There are several other things we can try to prevent ourselves falling prey to the vampire. Know your enemy! A psychic vampire can have a number of traits but more commonly the indicators are: ego, deceit, manipulation, self-centredness, greed, jealousy and resentfulness (the Seven 'Virtues' of a Vampire!). Moreover it is believed that they do not like poppy seeds and in European legend rosewood and hawthorn branches were used as stakes.

Defence and healing
You could create a vampire candle, either red or purple, with two drops each of the essential oils spikenard, vervain and basil and with two pinches of poppy seeds. Imagine protective mirrors coming up all around you like a shield, so that whatever is trying to harm you will bounce off the mirror and back to the vampire. Imagine your mirror shield as you say these words:

> *I know who you are.*
> *I know what you are.*
> *Stay away from me*
> *Now and forever.*
> *So mote it be.*

If you have had an attack then you need rest and healing. Light two white candles and place magic salt in a dish on your altar. Say these words:

> *Healing I need.*
> *Help me please.*
> *A victim I have been*

By one unseen.
Stars, send your healing to me.
An' it harm none, so mote it be.

Hold your hands up to the stars in a similar way to the image on the cover of this book, in a Y shape, and allow the healing energy of spirit to flow through you. Allow yourself to heal before commencing any other magical work.

The vampire is a part of spirit that we do not or do not want to recognise. Yet the day will overcome the night, and we learn from our experiences no matter how negative they may be. Keep strong and always keep your guard up.

Blessed Be

Werewolves

Dear Reader,

There has been much fiction written about werewolves, with many films and television series promoting their 'popularity'. Yet there is actually some truth wrapped up in the urban myths and legends of werewolves. There is a medical illness called lycanthropy[6] and those who suffer from this illness can to all intents and purposes behave like a wolf. The animal-like sounds that some people can make are very real. Also, a word of warning, that certain sessions of self-hypnosis have induced behaviour like a wolf in some people.

Throughout the world there are countless stories of werewolves. There are many sayings and customs pertaining to them such as in Greece where it is believed that eyebrows meeting above the nose indicate a werewolf. In Britain we have our own similar saying: 'Beware of those who eyebrows meet, for in their hearts lies deceit' (though this really just means that they are not to be trusted). This just shows how our appearance can be misinterpreted for so many things. Other indicators of a werewolf are said to be claw-like fingers and small pointed ears. It is also often said that the curse of the werewolf runs in families, which is interesting as some forms of illness are hereditary (perhaps lycanthropy?). We recreate what we know. Yet once again all of this relates to old customs.

---

[6] Lycanthropy has variously been linked with porphyria, hypertrichosis and rabies.

Nevertheless, in a recent poll over eighty per cent of people believed that werewolves once existed, proof that people believe in forms of spirit. Further, werewolves are not necessarily evil anyway. Wolves themselves are not the human-eating soul-destroying beings we are led to believe; in truth, wolves are actually very wary of humans and will not come near us. It is only when they are very hungry or very cold that they will wander close to a town. Unfortunately, people still go out and shoot them but actually there are more recorded fox attacks than wolf attacks in the world.

Some people believe that werewolves are nothing more than people dressed up in animal skins or those under the influence of hallucinogenic drugs, a bit like the flying witches of yore. Certain hallucinogenic drugs can indeed give the sensation of having hairy skin. Belladonna is one of them and belladonna would have been one of the key plants many people would have used for various things in past times.

One persistent tale about werewolves is that if you have the misfortune to become one it is said that the affliction will only last for nine years and will then leave you. However, if while in that state you hurt anyone or eat any human flesh then you will remain a werewolf for eternity.

There are many ways in which a person might become a werewolf. One of them is by heredity, in which case there is nothing much you can do about it. Another is that you are bitten by a werewolf, in which case do not eat anyone for nine years and then you will be fine! Of course, the other way you might become a werewolf is due to an enchantment or spell by a witch. Yes, blame the witches again! People believed that the witches' spells could be broken if you pointed at the victim in their human form and shouted, 'You are the wolf!' three times. Failing that, you would call out their Christian name three times while they are in their wolf form. Failing that, run!

However, as with all bad witches' spells of the past, if you did try to break the spell there is always the possibility that the curse could transfer onto you…

There is something generic in all these stories and customs concerning werewolves. In every country and in every culture, the practice that they have in common is shape-shifting. A werewolf, by however they got there, is nothing more than a shape-shifter. There are countless stories of shape-shifting gods and goddesses, shamans and medicine men. The possibility of shape-shifting, of transforming yourself into something else, has been written about since the beginning of time. You can take on many of the attributes of the animal of your choice - the strength of a bear, the ferociousness of a lion, the stealth of a snake, the wisdom of an owl or the independence of a lone wolf.

To help you decide on which animal characteristic you would like to have, use the zodiac of the Native Americans. The Medicine Wheel is extremely fascinating and very deep, with many layers and levels of understanding. It has an outer wheel that is divided into twelve birth periods, each with its own animal totem complete with stone, tree and colour affinities. These animal totems help you to connect to the power abilities they represent.

Goose	December 22nd - January 19th
Otter	January 20th - February 18th
Wolf	February 19th - March 20th
Falcon	March 21st - April 19th
Beaver	April 20th - May 20th
Deer	May 21st - June 20th
Woodpecker	June 21st - July 21st
Salmon	July 22nd - August 21st
Brown bear	August 22nd - September 21st

Crow September 22nd - October 22nd

Snake October 23rd - November 22nd

Owl November 23rd - December 21st

(These dates are for the northern hemisphere; for the southern, add six months.)

As always with spiritual matters, if you are attracted to the wonder of the Sioux, Navajo, Hopi and all the other magnificent native peoples of America, then research them and you may realise you have been called home. The Medicine Wheel year is extremely intricate, but see which animal you are connected to. Each of these animals has a set of specific characteristics that will come naturally to you too. For example, those who are born under the sign of the wolf value freedom and their own space; they are also very artistic people and extremely sensitive, but never break their trust or you may just see the wolf.

On your altar, you could have a specific image of your animal totem that you could use to meditate on and gain strength from. In addition, if you are a wolf or you would like to connect with your inner wolf (or werewolf) then there are a number of stones you could use. Howlite is a wonderful little stone and it is helpful for those who have problems sleeping. The other stone is of course moonstone; this translucent stone shimmers with yellow streaks when you hold it up to the light. But the best to use when connecting with your inner animal guide or spirit has to be the Norwegian moonstone, which is also called larvakite. This is quite an unassuming little stone with a wealth of power, so never underestimate it. It is a black-grey stone with iridescent colour flashes of silvery blue. It is the perfect stone for relating to the moon and for all those who love the moon for whatever reason - and not just for howling at either!

Enjoy connecting with your inner animal. Once again, please remember that no animal is evil in the Craft. No animal deserves to be destroyed just because it is doing entirely what it was made for. We all have a purpose and we all have a right to be here. We are all spirit. We are all one.

Blessed Be

Conclusion

Dear Reader,

We have now come to the end of our journey through the Craft. Each of the books in this series has brought something different to our exploration of the Craft. We have looked at festivals in the Turning of the Wheel of the Year in *The Craft in the City*, while in *The Witch in the City* I described the specific life festivals that we all go through in our life journey. In *Spells in the City* we have learned how to create our own spells, while in *Magic in the City* we have discovered the magic that is deep within us and flows through nature and is all around us at all times. Finally, here in *Spirit in the City* we have learned about the many different elementals of spirit that we can work with (or choose to avoid). If we could condense these books down into one-word meanings, it would be as follows:

Craft	Enjoy
Witch	Learn
Spells	Create
Magic	Participate
Spirit	Believe

Like our sacred sign of the pentagram, the five books of this series echo the Craft itself, with the message that it is within and all around you. Spirit is about belief.

We do not have to go to great expense to practise the Craft as nature will supply most of what we need. In this book we have looked at some different crystals yet we really do not have to pay a fortune for them. In the British Isles, we have a veritable treasure trove of possibilities; there are so many naturally occurring crystals and gem stones that really every county can give us what we need.

Along the coastline of Kent you can find anything from coins to Baltic amber, while the best place to find amber is along the Suffolk coastline. Whitby has the best jet in the world and the East Sussex beaches have many crystals and stones that are mentioned in this book. We have nearly a hundred miles of coastline from Devon to Dorset that has fossils and other goodies to find, similar to 'the Dinosaur Coast' of East Yorkshire. Ireland is perfect for finding quartz all along its beaches. Scotland is a treasure trove of naturally occurring gems, such as quartz, gold, sapphires, jasper, agates, citrine, serpentine marble, amethyst and Scottish pearls, which were highly prized in Roman times.

These are just some of the naturally formed treasures, yet the manmade ones of the British Isles are just as magical. Our history and culture is full of Viking, Celtic, Anglo-Saxon and Roman influences and the treasures of those times are still sleeping beneath the land we walk upon. The coasts around Cornwall yield some of the most beautiful sea glass in the world. You can use this to decorate a mermaid mirror, for example.

Never go to great expense to practise the Craft - if you need something it will find you eventually. Spirit will deliver. All the elementals and the other aspects of spirit mentioned in this book are here to guide and teach us in some way. Yet we are as much a part of spirit as those we have looked at. Humans are the physical manifestation of spirit within this time and space. No matter what happens, we shall always be here in this moment.

It is because of how special and truly unique we are that we are able to connect to spirit. We can realise that magic is a part of the whole and through the Craft we can connect once more with one another. We adapt, we grow, we change but those who practise the Craft will always be here.

We are spirit. And we BELIEVE.

So mote it be.

The Festivals and their Elementals

Imbolc	The Lady of the Lake, leprechauns *February 2nd – the arrival of the spring*
Ostara	Merfolk, angels *March 20th – the spring equinox*
Beltane	Nymphs, dragons, salamanders *May 1st – the festival of fertility*
Litha	Fairies, pixies, elves *June 20th - midsummer solstice*
Lammas	Unicorns, Pegasus *August 1st – the first festival of autumn*
Mabon	Sphinx *September 22nd – the Harvest Festival*
Samhain	Vampires, werewolves, serpents *October 31st – Hallowe'en, New Year*
Yule	Phoenix *December 20th - midwinter*

Other Magical Beings of Spirit

Here are some other beings and manifestations of spirit. There are many more but for this list the number of reported sightings and the overall awareness of them were deciding factors. In many counties and states, cultures and countries, there are other beings whose legends we have grown up with (such as the Red Dwarf of Detroit). We may have even encountered them ourselves. But as written previously, never be afraid for you are of spirit too and this is your time and your dimension; just be respectful if you encounter another form of spirit.

Blessed Be

Alien

An unknown entity that could be inner- or extra-terrestrial in origin. Encounters with aliens outnumber all recorded meetings with other beings of spirit. Friend or foe, physical or spiritual, the jury is still out. Yet those who have encounters with them often claim that their spirituality has developed further.

Banshee

An Irish spirit who wanders the ghostly plane. Her cries of pain are a terrifying scream as she calls souls to her. She is often thought to be an omen of death and doom.

Bunyip

A creature from aboriginal legend. The Bunyip lives in swamps, lakes and rivers of the Australian outback, and is known for bringing disease.

Dover Demon

The Crow tribe of America believed the Mannegishi are trickster spirits. They look almost human with large eyes and tiny bodies. They have been seen in Massachusetts, USA, and have become known as Dover Demons.

Genies

Genies can be found in all cultures in one form or another. Yet they generally stem from one in particular, the Middle East, where they are called Jinn. They are spiritual creatures who have the ability to grant mortals three wishes if we release them, usually from a lamp. Genies are known to be tricksters so always be careful with them; as with all magic, you need to be specific in what you are asking for!

Gremlins

Gremlins dwell in places where there is machinery of all types. They generally just like to tinker with it and play with tools. They can be a nuisance but are not evil.

Imps

Imps are rather bad little beings and very similar to gremlins, but imps are very evil and generally do the bidding of their master, the angel who fell from grace.

The imp is the symbol of the medieval city of Lincoln and the Lincolnshire Imp is a delightful story of good overcoming bad.

One day, two imps were doing the bidding of their master Satan by causing mayhem, such as smashing tables and chairs and even tripping up the Bishop. When an angel who was having none of this behaviour, especially in Lincoln Cathedral, told them off, in typical impish fashion one of them retaliated and turned him into stone, which is how he has remained to this day. If you ever go to Lincoln please do visit the cathedral and see if you can find him. Yet what of the other imp, you may ask? Well, he ran away to Grimsby and began to repeat his behaviour of causing mayhem. At this point the angel reappeared and gave the imp a good beating on the backside before turning him into stone too. You can still see this imp rubbing his bottom in St James' Church in Grimsby.

However the Lincolnshire Imp is actually three imps; there are two in Lincoln and one in the north-east of Lincolnshire. See if you can find the third one!

Jersey Devil

The Jersey Devil of America has a number of recorded sightings across all centuries. The earliest legends date back to the Native American tribes of the area. To all intents and purposes, the Jersey Devil is a dragon. If you do see it, do not approach it as it is extremely dangerous.

Lobs

Similar to the Brownie of Scotland, he is actually called a Lubber Fiend and is thought to be the product of a witch and the Devil. However, he is actually very nice and not at all evil - he will do household chores for you and all he would like in return is a saucer of milk.

If you have enjoyed this book, you will like...

The Craft in the City
First in this series, *The Craft in the City* will teach you everything you need to know about witchcraft in the modern world. Here, the essentials of the Craft and of Wiccan beliefs are condensed into a series of easy-to-read letters, in which the author describes spell-weaving, candle magic, the nature of ritual, how to make potions and much more. (ISBN 978-1-907203-43-5)

The Witch in the City
Tudorbeth teaches, in her simple and down-to-earth letters, what it really means to be a witch today. Here she unfolds the secrets of Bell, Book and Candle and of the mystical pentagram. She opens up to us the ceremonies of Initiation and Hand Fasting, and much more. (ISBN 978-1-907203-63-3)

Spells in the City
Who has not lit a candle for a loved one, or offered up a devout wish for some important event? Who has not believed in some lucky charm or spoken an affirmation? We are all practitioners of the Craft! So would you like to know how to do it properly, with real natural power and intent, and to get results? In this ground-breaking book, Tudorbeth opens up the traditional secrets of spell-weaving and adapts them for our busy modern lives as never seen before. More than one hundred real and practical spells for you to use now. (ISBN 978-1-907203-70-1)

Magic in the City

In this astonishing book, the fourth in her acclaimed series, Tudorbeth teaches us the traditional secrets of numerology and herbalism, how to read tea leaves and how to invite the gods and goddesses to bring miracles into our everyday lives. This ancient knowledge has never before been offered with such simplicity and clarity. (ISBN 978-1-907203-81-7)

Further details and extracts of these and many other beautiful titles may be seen at
www.local-legend.co.uk

Lightning Source UK Ltd.
Milton Keynes UK
UKOW05f1321270317
297606UK00008B/426/P